Front Porch Faith
Southern Lessons for the Soul
Charles E. Cravey

In His Steps Publishing

ISBN: (Paperback) 978-1-58535-041-4

ISBN: (Kindle) 978-1-58535-106-0

Library of Congress Catalog Number: 2025915749

Printed in the United States of America

Published by In His Steps Publishing

Contents

Preface
Why the Porch Still Matters

I didn't set out to write a book. I set out to remember.

To remember the quiet lessons learned on porches—mine and others. To remember the sacred hush of a rocking chair, the healing power of a shared meal, and the way grace shows up in ordinary places.

Front Porch Faith was born from those memories. From the stories that shaped me. From the people who loved me without needing to fix me. From the Spirit who whispered truth in the breeze.

This book is not a theological treatise. It's a front porch conversation. It's a mason jar of grace passed from my hand to yours. It's a place to sit, breathe, and remember that faith doesn't always shout—it often rocks slowly and waits for you to notice.

If you've ever felt weary, unseen, or unsure of your place in the world, I hope these pages feel like home. I hope they remind you that you are not forgotten. That you are not alone. That Grace still waits on the porch.

So, pull up a chair. Pour something sweet. And let's listen together.

The porch light is on.

The Rev. Dr. Charles E. Cravey, July 2025

1

Grace Between
the Rockers

"You will be like a well-watered garden, like a spring whose waters never fail." — Isaiah 58:11 (KJV)

This verse paints a vivid picture of abundance and renewal, offering a promise of continual nourishment and vitality. It evokes the image of a flourishing garden, thriving and vibrant, where every element is in harmony. In life, such a garden symbolizes personal growth, spiritual fulfillment, and enduring hope. The metaphor of a spring whose waters never fail suggests an eternal source of strength and sustenance, reassuring us that even in challenging times, we can draw upon inner reserves to flourish and thrive. This message of resilience and hope encourages us to cultivate our lives with care and intention, nurturing our spirits and those around us.

*****

Some days, grace doesn't thunder—it creaks quietly beneath you in a rocking chair worn smooth by time. The front porch becomes sacred not for its wood and nails, but for its spirit. On these plank-lined havens, neighbors pass by, and stories flow like sweet tea. You learn that presence is the truest hospitality. When you slow your pace long enough to listen, grace comes unannounced—sometimes holding sorrow, sometimes laughter, always bearing the weight of welcome.

Here, the porch is not just architecture—it is an altar. It is where the divine reclines in evening light, whispering healing in the hush.

Southern Hospitality: Grace Served on a Plate

"Do not forget to show hospitality to strangers, for by so doing some have entertained angels unawares." — Hebrews 13:2 (KJV)

In the South, hospitality isn't an event—it's a rhythm. It lives in casseroles assembled from memory and in hand-me-down teacups filled with sweetness. It appears when your neighbor weeps on the steps and you offer nothing but a chair and a quiet ear.

Hospitality is spiritual. It's holy ground disguised as mismatched chairs and wide front porches. It is grace, ladled into bowls and passed without judgment.

I remember Grandma Cravey—never hurried, never schooled, yet always prepared to feed whomever the Lord sent. Her porch was cathedral-like. Her table was communion.

Legacy and Life Lesson

Sometimes the front porch teaches louder than pulpits. One day, I sat beside Mr. Ransom, a man whose sermons came in silence. He listened more than he spoke. When I asked how he kept faith steady, he smiled slowly and said,

"Son, I just keep the rocking chair in motion and let God do the talking."

His words didn't rise like thunder—but like dew on the morning grass. That was grace unspoken, and it changed me.

Historical Porch Culture

Throughout Southern history, porches have been more than aesthetic—they've been communal sanctuaries. They were once our radios, our pulpits, and our confessionals. Voices would drift into twilight with hymns, laughter, and memory. Generations passed down wisdom not through lectures but through stories cradled in the wind. Faith didn't need amplification—it just needed a place to rest.

As a child, I can clearly remember our front porch "services" on Sunday afternoons when neighbors would come together. Some would play instruments, while others sang cherished old gospel songs. We lacked a radio, television, internet, or Facebook, yet we stayed informed about the world through one another. Oh, how we long for those days once more!

Porch Psalm

Blessed are they who linger in the light,

Whose chairs sway to the rhythm of heaven.

Their voices are low, but their welcome wide.

God meets them in the murmurs, not the miracles.

Reader Reflection

- When has grace shown up for you in a quiet place?

- Who has offered you porch hospitality when you needed it most?

- Where is your personal rocking chair moment with God?

Porch Gospel Snapshot

In Luke 10, we find Jesus at the home of Martha and Mary. One prepares, one listens—but both encounter the sacred on their doorstep. The moment isn't framed in grandeur. It's intimate, messy, and human.

Much like the porch, that room was cluttered with ordinary life—and yet it held eternity. In stillness, Mary found her place. And perhaps the porch, too, is a place where the better portion can still be chosen.

It is a space where the divine meets the daily, where the sacred dances with the mundane. Just as Mary chose to sit at the feet of Jesus, we are invited to pause, to listen, and to embrace the holiness that dwells in simplicity.

On porches across the South, much like in that biblical home, the clatter of dishes and the hum of everyday duties mingle with the whispers of grace. Here, there are no demands to be someone else or somewhere else. Instead, there is a gentle call to be present, to let time stretch, and to find solace in the gentle sway of a rocking chair.

In this quietude, we are reminded that life's richest moments often come not in the grand gestures but in the quiet conversations and shared silences. The porch transforms into a sacred space where hearts are unburdened and souls find rest.

So, may we all find our porch moments—places where we can choose the better portion, where we can sit, listen, and be transformed by the grace that waits patiently for us to notice.

Southern Wisdom

"The best portion of a good man's life: his little, nameless, unremembered acts of kindness and love." — William Wordsworth

These quiet gestures often go unnoticed, yet they leave an indelible mark on the hearts they touch. Whether it's a simple smile to a stranger, a comforting word to a friend, or a helping hand to those in need, these small acts create ripples of goodness that extend far beyond their moment.

In a world that can sometimes feel overwhelming, it's these acts of kindness that remind us of our shared humanity and the profound impact we can have on each other's lives.

"Hospitality is love in action. It's the Gospel served warm." — Southern Proverb

This saying embodies the essence of Southern hospitality, where welcoming guests is more than a tradition—it's a heartfelt practice rooted in kindness and generosity. Whether it's sharing a meal, offering a comforting word, or simply opening one's home, this warmth fosters a sense of belonging and community. In every act of hospitality, there is an opportunity to connect, to share stories, and to create lasting memories that enrich the lives of both the host and the guest.

The Porch Where Mercy Waits

Charles E. Cravey

Where silence rocks in time with broken need,
And stillness speaks what hurried hearts forget—
The porch becomes a holy, hushed retreat
Where souls uncoil from trials and regret.

A breeze might carry prayer upon its wing.
Unspoken words that ache to be believed.
Sweet tea and hymnals gently start to sing
Of sacred joy the world has not conceived.

So come and sit. Don't worry what you bring.
No mask is needed, no parade, no name—
Just be. Be held beneath the Spirit's wing
Until you feel what grace has come to claim.

The porch still waits. The chair still sways in tune.
And mercy rocks beneath the Southern moon.

Prayer Bench Moment

Lord, slow me down until my soul catches up.

Let me rest on the porch of your presence,

Where grace moves gently and love listens long.

May my welcome be wide, my heart at ease,

And my rocking chair in tune with yours. Amen.

Porchlight Parable

Grace doesn't shout.
It rocks slowly and waits for you to notice.

In the quiet corners of Southern life, the porch stands as a timeless sentinel of welcome and warmth. It invites without words, offering the solace of shared silence and the gentle hum of togetherness. As fireflies begin their nightly dance and the cicadas sing their evening hymns, the porch becomes a bridge between the mundane and the divine, a place where time slows down just enough for the soul to breathe.

Here, beneath the broad sky and swaying trees, the simplest moments become profound. A shared glance, a knowing nod, or the comforting rhythm of a rocking chair can speak volumes. The porch is a keeper of secrets and a cradle of hope, where the past and present mingle, and the future feels a little less daunting.

In this sacred space, grace isn't an abstract concept—it's a lived experience, woven into the fabric of everyday life. It finds expression in the laughter of children playing in the yard, in the gentle admonitions of a grandmother, and in the quiet strength of those who gather to simply be together. The porch is a testament to the power of presence, a reminder that sometimes, just being there is the greatest gift of all.

So, when the world feels too fast and too loud, remember the porch. Let it be a sanctuary of peace, a place where grace patiently waits to be found and where love is always ready to welcome you home.

2

Holy Ground
Where You're Planted

"And he said, draw not nigh hither: put off thy shoes from off thy feet, for the place whereon thou standest is holy ground." — Exodus 3:5 (KJV)

There are moments when God breaks into the ordinary—when dirt becomes sacred, when silence burns, and when a front porch becomes as holy as the mountain before the bush. Moses wasn't on a pulpit. He was tending sheep. And yet God showed up.

What makes a place holy isn't its grandeur—it's the presence of the Almighty. It's the whisper that says, "You are not alone." Sometimes, the sacred wraps itself in sunlight on a cracked wooden floor or in a whispered prayer at the edge of your garden bed.

I've stood in pulpits and on porches. But the most sacred places I've known have often come when I wasn't looking—when grace found me feet-first, weathered and weary, right where I was planted.

And in those unexpected moments, I have learned to pause, to breathe, and to recognize the holy ground beneath my feet. Life has a way of weaving the divine into the fabric of the everyday, transforming the mundane into a tapestry of wonder. It is in the quiet, unassuming spaces that the sacred often whispers its loudest truths, inviting us to listen with open hearts and open minds.

Whether it's the laughter shared around a dinner table, the comforting embrace of a loved one, or the simple act of kindness from a stranger, these are the altars where the soul finds solace and strength. Here, the ordinary becomes extraordinary, and we are reminded that the divine is not confined to the grandiose but is present in the gentle embrace of the now.

Grandma's Garden

My grandmother—whose prayers weighed more than sermons—once led me to her humble garden behind the house. Her fingers dug into the soil like she was searching for God. And in a way, she was.

"I talk to Him here," she said, brushing dirt from her palms. "He answers while I wait. Sometimes in silence."

That garden was holy ground. Not because of miracle harvests, but because heaven hovered when she planted, prayed, and waited.

I've come to believe that anywhere soaked with obedience becomes sacred. Whether it's soil, a rocking chair, or a place between sorrows—when you stand in surrender, holiness settles there.

Faith in the Ordinary

Holy ground often appears in places we ignore. The quiet pew in the back of the church. The car ride that holds your heartache. The hallway you pace when news hasn't yet come.

We think sacredness belongs in lofty moments. But God etched it into simple places. Into porches. Into the rhythm of coffee poured for a stranger. Into a phone call made to ask forgiveness.

Holiness isn't staged. It's incarnated. And it calls us to take off our shoes and see the divine in the dusty moments.

In the embrace of a shared silence, holiness whispers
its presence, inviting us to find grace in the mundane. It is in the laughter shared over a dinner table,
the gentle touch of a hand on a weary shoulder, and
the soft glow of a lamp illuminating a quiet evening
spent with loved ones. These moments, seemingly
ordinary, are where the sacred unfurls its wings and
takes flight. It is here, amid the everyday chaos and
calm, that we are reminded of the beauty that exists
in simply being present.

In our hurried lives, we often overlook these hallowed spaces, seeking grandeur when the divine is
right under our noses. Each step we take on this
earth is a dance with the sacred, a chance to encounter the holy in the most unexpected corners of
our lives. So let us tread lightly, with open hearts and
eyes wide to the wonders of the world around us,
embracing the extraordinary within the ordinary.

Southern Wisdom

"Earth's crammed with heaven, and every common bush afire with God.
But only he who sees takes off his shoes." — Elizabeth Barrett Browning

"Wherever God dwells, the soil becomes sanctuary."
— Anonymous

The Ground That Glows

Charles E. Cravey

He spoke through flame but did not burn the tree,
And Moses knelt on soil that dared to shine.
The holy danced in dirt and mystery,
A hush that held the echo of divine.

No temple built by hands was present there.

No choir sang; no veil was drawn aside.

Just feet and fire, trembling in the air—

A place where heaven did not need to hide.

So too the porch, the garden, and the field,

Where grace and gravel meet beneath the sky.

There holiness is gently, sweetly sealed

When one draws near, unshod, with humbled cry.

The sacred waits in places small and sound—

And every yielded step becomes God's ground.

Prayer Bench Moment

Lord, may I never miss your presence wrapped in
quiet.

Let me see holy ground not just in temples,

But in my garden, my porch, my pain.

Wherever you call me to stand,

Let me take off my shoes—and my pride.

Make me aware. Make me tender. Make me yours.

Amen.

Reader Reflection

- Where have you unexpectedly encountered sacredness?

- What ordinary places feel spiritually significant in your life?

- Are you willing to let your present location become holy ground?

Porchlight Parable

The ground isn't holy because you planned it.
It's holy because He showed up.

In the quiet moments before dawn, when the world
is still wrapped in the gentle embrace of night, there
is a sacredness that permeates the air. It is in these
hushed hours that the porchlight flickers to life,
casting a warm glow on the steps where countless
stories have unfolded. This is where the ordinary
meets the extraordinary—a place where whispered
prayers and heartfelt confessions have mingled with
the cool morning breeze.

Each creak of the floorboards and rustle of the leaves
tells a tale of its own. It's not the meticulously laid
plans or the carefully arranged decor that sanctify
this space; it's the unexpected encounters, the moments of grace and revelation that transform it into

hallowed ground. Here, under the watchful gaze of the stars, souls find solace, and the divine presence makes itself known in ways both subtle and profound.

As the first light of daybreak begins to paint the sky in hues of pink and gold, the porch becomes a bridge between the dreams of night and the realities of day. It's a reminder that holiness is not confined to grand cathedrals or lofty ideals; it can be found in the simple, everyday moments where love, hope, and faith converge.

3

Connect the Dots

The Treasure is Discovered at the End

"In all thy ways acknowledge him, and he shall direct thy paths." — Proverbs 3:6 (KJV)

We spend so much of life trying to make sense of scattered dots—moments, wounds, triumphs, losses. At first glance, they seem unrelated. A broken friendship in youth. A near miss on the highway. A random compliment that changed your career. Each event feels like a solitary speck on life's canvas.

But then Grace begins to connect them. Slowly. Tenderly. Like a loving hand guiding a child's crayon between numbered stars. And suddenly, what you thought was random sorrow becomes radiant symmetry. Every step, every misstep—even the quiet in-between places—has led to the unveiling of your divine design.

And here's the wonder: the treasure revealed isn't what you do. It's who you are. You are God's masterpiece—hidden in plain sight, uncovered in grace.

A Cravey Family Dot

I remember a moment when the dots aligned in my own life—not with fanfare, but with quiet conviction. My calling to write didn't come with fireworks. It came one morning as I sat on the porch and read an old letter from my aunt. In it, she quoted Proverbs 3:5–6 and told me, "Son, every step counts."

That day, I looked back—at ministry, marriage, children, sorrow, and creativity—and saw something I hadn't before: that even my waiting seasons were not wasted. They were brushstrokes in the portrait of who God had crafted me to be.

I wasn't trying to be something. I was becoming someone.

When the Picture Appears

Most of us want clarity from the start. But faith isn't about control—it's about trust. Like that old connect-the-dots puzzle we once filled out as children, the picture doesn't make sense until all the numbers are joined.

God rarely gives us the full image at the beginning. But He does give the next number. And with each faithful step, the shape of our calling emerges: not rushed, but revealed.

And when it's all said and done, you won't just see a masterpiece. You'll realize—you were the treasure hidden in the design all along.

Southern Wisdom

"God don't waste nothing—not even broken porch steps."

Grace does not show you the full map—it simply offers the next step. Inspired by Charles Spurgeon

Lines of Grace

Charles E. Cravey

They placed the dots in scattered, lonely ways,
Like stars too far to form a sky complete.
I wept, unsure of why the pain would stay,
Or how my soul could stand without defeat.

But slowly He began to guide my hand,
A line from sorrow curving into praise.
And all the things I didn't understand
Became the path that brought me through the maze.

Now every mark, once random and apart,
Connects with others in a holy thread.
A portrait drawn by grace upon my heart,
A story only heaven could have read.

The treasure isn't found in what I write—
It's that He saw me always in His light.

Prayer Bench Moment

Lord, help me not to rush the picture.

Give me courage to draw each line with trust,

even when I can't see the next curve.

Reveal your grace not only in the finished image,

but in the act of becoming. Amen.

Reader Reflection

- What moments in your life once felt random or wasted?

- How might they connect under God's hand today?

- Can you trust the next dot, even if the whole picture's not clear yet?

Porchlight Parable

The treasure wasn't buried.
You were just learning how to see it.

Each day, as the sun dipped below the horizon, the porchlight flickered on, casting a warm, inviting glow over the worn wooden steps. It was here, in this unassuming spot, that countless stories had unfolded. Neighbors would gather, laughter mingling with the soft hum of crickets, as moments turned into memories.

This porch was more than just a place; it was a haven, a testament to the simple joys that life offers when we take the time to notice. The treasure, after all, wasn't gold or jewels—it was the shared smiles, the heartfelt conversations, and the comforting presence of friends and family. It was love, in its most genuine and accessible form, waiting patiently for those who chose to pause and appreciate its brilliance.

4

A Foreigner in a Foreign Land
Grace in the Land of Strangers

"These all died in faith, not having received the promises, but having seen them afar off... and confessed that they were strangers and pilgrims on the earth." — Hebrews 11:13 (KJV)

There's a weight to not quite belonging. Moses knew it. Born Hebrew, raised Egyptian, caught between bloodline and empire. He wandered not just through deserts, but through identity itself.

In today's world, many Christians feel the same dissonance. We walk roads paved with worldly priorities, yet yearn for heavenly truth. We are often foreigners—even in our hometowns—not because we choose isolation, but because our calling draws us out.

Being set apart is not loneliness. It is purpose. It means God is shaping us beyond comfort zones, calling us into spaces where obedience outweighs convenience.

Moses Between Worlds

Scripture tells us Moses was drawn from the water—his very name carried duality. He was cradled by Egyptian royalty yet destined to confront Pharaoh in the name of Israel. His split identity didn't disqualify him; it prepared him.

At the burning bush, God didn't ask Moses to clean up his confusion first. He just called him by name.

The porch, too, can be such a place—where we sit with discomfort, tangled roots, and unknowns, and still hear the whisper: *I know who you are. You are mine.*

Identity in a Fractured World

Being a Christian in this age can feel like standing in Egypt with a Hebrew soul. Our faith doesn't always blend in. We struggle to speak peace in polarized times. We feel the ache of being misread, misunderstood, or overlooked.

But perhaps that ache is holy. Perhaps it's proof that we were never made for shallow waters. We were made for calling, for wilderness wonder, for a deep and abiding walk that is less about where we are and more about who walks with us.

Timely Quotes

"For here have we no continuing city, but we seek one to come." — Hebrews 13:14 (KJV)

"Thou shalt be unto me a peculiar treasure above all people." — Exodus 19:5 (KJV)

To be called by God often means being misunderstood by man. — Inspired by Thomas à Kempis

"God made me Southern so I could understand grace between biscuits."

Between Two Names

Charles E. Cravey

He bore the robe of Pharaoh's gilded house,
Yet heard the cries of kin beneath the weight.
A Hebrew heart beneath a royal blouse,
A story caught between two hands of fate.

He wandered not just sand, but soul and name,
Unsure which voice would finally guide his feet.
But burning bushes never play at games—
They beckon us where earth and heaven meet.

And though the world may dress you in disguise,
And culture press you into borrowed ways,
God calls by name—not mask, not worldly ties—
And leads you through identity's dismays.

The porch still welcomes pilgrims passing through,
With chairs that hold both heritage and hue.

Prayer Bench Moment

Lord, when I feel like a stranger—even in familiar
places—remind me that you are not confused by my
heart.
Speak my name again. Call me as you did Moses.
Not by my labels, but by your love.

Let my porch become a place of belonging, even when the world feels foreign. Amen.

Reader Reflection

- Have you ever felt "in-between" in life or faith?

- What parts of your story carry tension between past and future?

- What would it mean to let God name you instead of culture or circumstance?

Porchlight Parable

You're not misplaced.

You're on your way to purpose—and that's a holy kind of in-between.

Embrace this moment as a cocoon of growth, where your potential is quietly unfurling. Trust the journey, even when the path seems uncertain, for it is in these moments of transition that the most profound transformations occur.

Like a butterfly emerging from its chrysalis, you are in the process of becoming something beautiful and resilient. Allow yourself the grace to evolve, and remember that every step forward, no matter how small, is a step towards the light of your true calling.

5

"Here I Am"
The Power of Showing Up for God

"Also I heard the voice of the Lord, saying, 'Whom shall I send, and who will go for us?' Then said I, Here am I; send me." — Isaiah 6:8 (KJV)

Obedience doesn't always arrive polished. It often shows up barefoot, trembling, and unsure. Isaiah didn't say, "I have the qualifications." He said, "Here I am." And heaven moved.

There is a sacred power in availability. In showing up before you know what the assignment is. The porch becomes a sanctuary of surrender—where the breeze invites stillness and the Spirit calls your name, not for your résumé, but for your willingness.

God doesn't look for polish. He looks for presence.

A Life of Availability

Some of the most transformative moments in my life came not because I planned well but because I was willing. A phone call answered at just the right time. A prayer whispered before I had the words. An "I'll go," uttered with a shaky heart.

You don't need a map to follow Jesus. You need a yes.

It was that yes that led Isaiah from unworthiness to divine commissioning. And it's that same yes that still reshapes souls on the front porch of faith today.

Every story of faith begins with a simple step, a moment of surrender where the heart opens to possibilities unseen. In Isaiah's story, his willingness to say "yes" transformed not only his life but also the lives of those he touched. It's a reminder that our journeys often start with the courage to step into the unknown, trusting that each step is guided by a purpose greater than ourselves.

The beauty of faith is that it doesn't require us to have all the answers. It asks only for our openness and a willingness to trust the journey. In the quiet moments, when doubt whispers and fear lingers, it's that unwavering "yes" that lights the path forward, illuminating the way one step at a time.

When God Whispers Your Name

The porch isn't just where we rest—it's where we respond. When God speaks, it's rarely a roar. More often, it's a stirring in the chest, a quiet urgency, a sentence in a devotional that won't let go.

Your role may not be the burning bush or the parted sea. It might be writing one letter. Making one visit. Opening your front door to someone aching for grace.

It starts when you say, *Here I am. I don't have all the answers—but I'm not hiding from the question.*

Timely Quotes

"I am only one, but I am one. I cannot do everything, but I can do something." — Edward Everett Hale

"Availability is the language of trust." — Inspired by Oswald Chambers

"God doesn't call the equipped. He equips the called." — Widely paraphrased truth

The Sound of Yes

Charles E. Cravey

He did not ask for answers from my soul,
Nor did He seek the strength I did not own.
He called me where my silence made me whole—
A whisper when I thought I stood alone.

He did not promise glory paved with gold,
Just grace to walk when shadows veiled the way.
He whispered, "Come," and all my fears grew
bold—
Yet Faith still chose to answer, not delay.

My "yes" was not a shout. It was a sigh.

A porch-bound prayer beneath a weeping moon.

But He received it like a sacred cry

And wrote it in His plan, a holy tune.

Here I am—not mighty, wise, or grand.

Just willing, Lord. Please take me as I stand.

Prayer Bench Moment

Lord, I may not know the way,

But I know the sound of Your voice.

When You call, let my soul rise like the morning,

not with answers, but with surrender.

I am not ready, but I am willing.

Here I am. Amen.

Reader Reflection

- What moment in your life opened when you simply said "yes"?

- Do you struggle with needing all the details before you obey?

- How might availability, not ability, lead you deeper into God's plan?

Porchlight Parable

God doesn't need your strength.
He needs your "yes"—spoken with a surrendered heart and willing feet.

Whether it's the gentle nudge to reach out to a friend in need or the unexpected opportunity to serve a stranger, it's in these moments of quiet obedience that the most profound transformations occur. Each "yes" is like a stone cast into a still pond, creating ripples that extend far beyond our own understanding.

It's in this sacred surrender where we find divine purpose, illuminating paths we never thought to walk and filling our hearts with a joy that only comes from knowing we are part of something greater than ourselves.

6

"Let My People Go!"

Freedom for the Weary Soul

"And afterward Moses and Aaron went in and told Pharaoh, 'Thus saith the Lord God of Israel, Let my people go, that they may hold a feast unto me in the wilderness.'" — Exodus 5:1 (KJV)

There comes a time when the soul grows tired—not from lack of faith, but from the weight of captivity. Today's Christian community is weary. Not because we've stopped believing, but because we've been carrying burdens we were never meant to bear.

Moses didn't ask Pharaoh for comfort. He asked for release. Not for luxury, but for liberty. God's people were not called to survive Egypt—they were called to leave it.

And so are we.

The Weight of Modern Captivity

We live in a world that demands performance, perfection, and constant motion. Even in faith circles, we often feel pressure to be "on fire," "sold out," or "radically available." But sometimes, the most spiritual thing you can do is rest.

Let my people go... from burnout.

Let my people go... from shame.

Let my people go... from the lie that they must earn grace.

The porch is a place of release. It's where we exhale. It's where we stop pretending and start healing.

A Personal Exodus

I remember a season when ministry felt more like a treadmill than a calling. I was doing all the right things—but my soul was tired. One afternoon, I sat on the porch and simply said, "Lord, I can't keep this pace."

And I felt the Spirit whisper, *"Then don't."*

That moment became my personal Exodus. I didn't leave the ministry—I left the mindset that God needed me to be exhausted to be effective. I stepped into a new rhythm. One of grace. One of rest. One of freedom.

Timely Quotes

"Come unto me, all ye that labour and are heavy laden, and I will give you rest." — Matthew 11:28 (KJV)

"God never asks us to run faster than grace can carry us." — Inspired by Andrew Murray

"Freedom is not the absence of struggle—it's the presence of peace." — Paraphrased truth

The Call to Release

Charles E. Cravey

He did not ask for comfort, gold, or fame,
But simply that the captives be set free.
A voice that trembled still declared His name,
And Pharaoh heard the echo of decree.

So too the soul that labors in disguise,
That wears a smile while aching deep within.

The Lord still speaks, and weary hearts arise—
Not to perform, but to be whole again.

Let go, He says, of burdens you've amassed.
Let go of guilt that grace has long erased.
Step out from Egypt—leave the shameful past,
And walk into the wilderness embraced.

The porch becomes a place of holy flight—
Where chains fall off beneath the morning light.

Prayer Bench Moment

Lord, I've carried too much for too long.

Let me hear Your voice again—

Not in thunder, but in release.

Break the chains I've accepted as normal.

Let me walk in freedom,

even if the path leads through wilderness.

I trust You to lead me out. Amen.

Reader Reflection

- What burdens have you been carrying that God never asked you to bear?

- Where do you need spiritual release—not escape, but freedom?

- Can you trust God to lead you through the wilderness into rest?

Porchlight Parable

Freedom doesn't always feel like a parade.
Sometimes it feels like finally breathing again.

The gentle rustle of leaves in the evening breeze whispered secrets of liberation, a reminder that freedom often arrives in quiet, unexpected moments. As the porchlight flickered softly, casting a warm glow over the familiar landscape, the world beyond seemed to stretch out endlessly, full of promise and new beginnings. In that serene space, the heart found solace, unshackled from the burdens of the day, embracing the stillness that enveloped everything. It was here, on this unassuming porch, that the true essence of freedom was felt—not in grand gestures, but in the simple act of being present and at peace.

7

Our "True" Identity

Identity

Becoming Who God Already Sees

"But ye are a chosen generation, a royal priesthood,
an holy nation, a peculiar people; that ye should shew

forth the praises of him who hath called you out of darkness into his marvellous light." — 1 Peter 2:9 (KJV)

We spend much of life trying to answer the question, *Who am I?* The world offers titles, roles, and reputations. But God offers something deeper—identity rooted in grace.

You are not your past.

You are not your performance.

You are not your pain.

You are chosen. You are beloved. You are called.

The Porch Mirror

There's something sacred about sitting on a porch and reflecting—not just on life, but on self. The rocking chair becomes a mirror. Not one that shows flaws, but one that reveals truth.

I remember a morning when I sat outside, wrestling with doubt. I had failed in something I cared about deeply. I felt unworthy. But as the sun rose and the breeze stirred, I sensed God whispering, *You are still mine.*

That moment didn't erase my failure. It redefined me beyond it.

The Labels We Wear

We wear many labels: parent, pastor, friend, failure, success. But none of them define us fully. God's identity for us is not based on what we do—it's based on who He is.

When Moses asked, "Who am I?" God didn't give a résumé. He gave a promise: *I will be with you.*

Your true identity is not found in your reflection. It's found in your relationship.

Timely Quotes

"Know thyself, and thou shalt know God." — Thomas à Kempis

"Our identity is not in what we achieve, but in what we receive." — Inspired by Henri Nouwen

"You are not what others see—you are what God declares." — Paraphrased truth

The Name He Gave

Charles E. Cravey

They called me by the names the world had
known—
Success and failure, titles worn and torn.
But none could reach the marrow or the bone
Where Grace had carved a name before I was born.

He whispered not what I had done or said.
But who I was beneath the masks I wore.

A child of light, though I had walked with dread,
A soul redeemed, though I had shut the door.

So now I sit upon this porch of peace,
No longer chasing mirrors made of man.
I rest in Him, and all my striving ceases—
For He has named me part of His great plan.

The name He gave is written in the skies:
Beloved, chosen, seen through heaven's eyes.

Prayer Bench Moment

Lord, strip away the names I've accepted that don't
belong to me.
Let me hear Your voice again—
the one that calls me child,
the one that calls me home.
May I live not from labels,
but from love. Amen.

Reader Reflection

- What names or labels have you carried that God never gave you?

- How does knowing you are chosen change the way you see yourself?

- What would it look like to live from identity, not insecurity?

Porchlight Parable

You are not becoming someone else.
You are becoming who God already sees.

As you journey through life, you are not crafting a new identity from scratch but rather unveiling the masterpiece that has always been within you. Each experience, each moment of growth, is like a gentle brushstroke, revealing the colors and textures that make you unique. Embrace the process with patience and grace, knowing that every step forward is a step toward the truest version of yourself. Let the light within you shine brightly, illuminating not only your path but also inspiring those around you to embark on their own journeys of self-discovery.

8

Sweet Tea Grace
The Gospel Served Cold and Sweet

"Be not forgetful to entertain strangers: for thereby some have entertained angels unawares." — Hebrews 13:2 (KJV)

In the South, sweet tea isn't just a beverage—it's a love language. It's poured without asking, offered without judgment, and served with a smile that says, *You belong here.*

Hospitality is holy. It's not about perfection—it's about presence. It's the Gospel in a mason jar. Grace doesn't always come with a sermon. Sometimes it comes with a second helping and a seat on the porch.

The Ministry of Welcome

I've seen lives changed not by eloquent preaching, but by quiet kindness. A neighbor who brought a pie during a hard season. A church member who sat beside someone new without needing to speak. A grandmother who kept an extra plate ready—just in case.

These moments are not small. They are sacred. They are the ministry of welcome.

Sweet tea grace is the kind that doesn't ask for credentials. It simply says, *Come on in. We're glad you're here.*

When Hospitality Heals

There was a time when I felt out of place—spiritually dry, emotionally worn. I visited a friend who didn't ask questions. He just handed me a glass of tea and said, "Sit a while."

That moment healed something in me. Not because of the tea, but because of the tenderness. I didn't need fixing. I needed fellowship.

Hospitality is healing. It reminds us that we are not alone. That we are seen. That we are welcome.

Timely Quotes

"Hospitality is not to change people, but to offer them space where change can take place." — Henri Nouwen

"Kindness is the oil that takes the friction out of life." — Inspired by Frederick Buechner

"Grace is best served with a smile and a seat." —
Paraphrased truth

The Table of Grace

Charles E. Cravey

No silver set, no linen pressed with care,
Just mason jars and chairs that creak with age.
Yet here I find the Gospel in the air—
A welcome written on the porch's page.

She pours the tea, not asking where I've been.
Not judging what I carry in my soul.
She simply smiles and lets the grace begin.
A sweetness steeped in love that makes me whole.

The table doesn't boast of wealth or fame,
But every seat is sacred, every bite.
For here, the feast is served in Jesus' name,
And every guest is bathed in porchlight's light.

So come and sit. The tea is cold and sweet.

And grace is waiting in your rocking seat.

Prayer Bench Moment

Lord, let my home be a haven,

my porch, a place of peace,

and my table a testimony of grace.

May I welcome others as You have welcomed me—

without condition, without hesitation,

with joy and with love. Amen.

Reader Reflection

- Who has shown you hospitality that felt like healing?

- How can you offer grace in simple, tangible ways?

- What does it mean to serve the Gospel with sweetness?

Porchlight Parable

Sometimes the most spiritual thing you can do is pour a glass of tea and listen.

Beneath the gentle glow of the porchlight, the world seemed to pause, offering a moment of stillness in the midst of life's hustle. The warmth of the tea cup seeped into her hands, grounding her in the present, while the soothing aroma enveloped her like a comforting embrace. As she sat there, the symphony of crickets serenaded the night, and a gentle breeze whispered secrets through the leaves.

In this quiet sanctuary, she allowed her mind to wander, reflecting on the day's events and the lessons they carried. It was in these unhurried moments that clarity often emerged, like stars appearing in the twilight sky. She realized that listening—to the world, to others, and to oneself—was an art, one that brought wisdom and understanding.

With each sip of tea, she felt gratitude for the simple joys and the profound connections that life offered. The porchlight flickered softly, casting a warm glow that felt like a beacon of peace. Here, under its watchful eye, she found solace, knowing that sometimes, the most spiritual journey begins right at home.

9

Mother Teresa's Porch
Holiness in the Small Things

"Inasmuch as ye have done it unto one of the least of these my brethren, ye have done it unto me." — Matthew 25:40 (KJV)

Mother Teresa didn't preach from pulpits. She preached from sidewalks, hospital beds, and the quiet corners of suffering. Her ministry was not loud—it was low. Not grand—it was grounded.

She taught us that holiness is not found in doing great things, but in doing small things with great love.

The porch, too, can be a place of sacred service. You don't need to travel the world to love well. Sometimes, the most Christlike thing you can do is notice someone's pain and sit beside it.

The Ministry of Presence

Mother Teresa once said, "If you want to change the world, go home and love your family." That kind of wisdom doesn't trend—it transforms.

I've seen lives shift not through programs, but through presence. A neighbor who checks in. A friend who shows up. A stranger who smiles.

The porch is a place where love lingers. Where compassion doesn't need credentials. Where ministry is measured not in numbers, but in nearness.

Serving Without Spotlight

We often think service must be visible to be valuable. But the Kingdom of God is built on unseen kindness. On prayers whispered in kitchens. On meals delivered without fanfare. On tears wiped without applause.

Mother Teresa's porch was the world. Ours may be smaller—but no less sacred.

When we serve in silence, heaven hears.

Timely Quotes

"Not all of us can do great things. But we can do small things with great love." — Mother Teresa

"Do not think that love, in order to be genuine, has to be extraordinary." — Mother Teresa

"Holiness is not in the task—it's in the tenderness."
— Inspired by her legacy

The Porch of Mercy

Charles E. Cravey

She walked where pain had settled in the dust,
And knelt where others dared not lay their hand.
She did not speak of power, fame, or trust—
She simply served and let the love expand.

So too the porch where mercy finds its place,
Where rocking chairs become a sacred pew.
No need for robes or titles to embrace—
Just hearts that beat with kindness, pure and true.

The smallest act—a meal, a prayer, a smile—
Can echo through eternity's great hall.
For love that lingers even for a while
Becomes the loudest sermon of them all.

So let me serve where silence holds the key,

And find my porch a place of sanctity.

Prayer Bench Moment

Lord, let me love without needing credit.

Let me serve without seeking the spotlight.

Make my porch a place of mercy,

where the hurting are held,

and the unnoticed are known.

Teach me the holiness of small things. Amen.

Reader Reflection

- Where can you serve quietly and faithfully today?

- Who in your life needs presence more than advice?

- What small act of love could become a holy offering?

Porchlight Parable

The greatest ministries often begin with a chair, a cup, and a heart that listens.

On a quiet street, where the hustle and bustle of the city faded into a gentle hum, there sat an old wooden chair on a porch. Its paint was chipped, and it creaked with the stories of countless visitors, each having paused to share a moment of their lives. Beside it, a simple cup of tea or coffee, steaming gently in the cool morning air, awaited those who needed warmth both inside and out.

But it wasn't the chair or the cup that made this porch special. It was the presence of a kind soul; someone whose heart was wide open to the world. This person understood that sometimes the most profound impact came not from grand gestures but from quiet moments of connection. They knew that in a world that often rushed past, taking the time to truly listen was a rare and precious gift.

People from all walks of life, drawn by an invisible thread, found themselves on that porch. They shared their dreams, their fears, their joys, and their sorrows, knowing they would be met with compassion and understanding. In this simple act of listening, the porch light became a beacon of hope, reminding everyone that they were not alone and that their stories mattered.

10

St. Francis and the Garden Gate

Finding God in the Quiet of Creation

"The heavens declare the glory of God; and the firma-ment sheweth his handywork." — Psalm 19:1 (KJV)

St. Francis didn't need stained glass to worship. He found God in birdsong, in sunlight, in the hush of trees. His prayers were not confined to chapels—they rose from gardens, fields, and forest paths.

Creation is not just scenery—it's sanctuary. The garden gate is not merely an entrance—it's an invitation. To slow down. To listen. To see the divine in the dew.

The Gospel of Simplicity

We often complicate faith with noise and structure. But St. Francis reminds us that holiness can be found in simplicity. In feeding birds. In planting seeds. In walking barefoot through morning mist.

I've found that some of my deepest spiritual moments happen not in sermons, but in silence. When I'm tending a garden. Watching a squirrel. Listening to the wind.

The earth is not just God's handiwork—it's His hymn.

Porchside Creation

The porch offers a front-row seat to the sacred. You don't need to travel far to see God's glory. It's in the way the light hits the leaves. In the rhythm of rain. In the way a flower opens without fanfare.

St. Francis would have loved the porch. It's a place where nature and soul meet. Where peace is not a concept—it's a breeze.

Timely Quotes

"What you are looking for is what is looking." — St. Francis of Assisi

"In everything, give thanks—for everything belongs to God." — Inspired by St. Francis

"Creation is God's first cathedral." — Paraphrased truth

The Garden Gate

Charles E. Cravey

He walked where lilies bowed without a sound,
And sang with sparrows praises to the skies.
He found the sacred not in vaulted ground,
But in the hush where humble beauty lies.

So too the porch, where petals preach with grace,
And breezes carry whispers of the Lord.
No need for robes or rituals to chase—
Just hearts that hear what silence has outpoured.

The garden gate swings open to the soul,
Inviting peace where chaos used to reign.
And every leaf becomes a sacred scroll,
A sermon written in the morning rain.

So let me walk with Francis through the dew.

And find my faith in all that God makes new.

Prayer Bench Moment

Lord, let me see You in the quiet.

In the garden. In the breeze. In the bird's song.

Teach me to worship not just with words,

but with wonder.

Let my porch become a place of peace,

where creation speaks and my soul listens. Amen.

Reader Reflection

- Where in nature have you felt closest to God?

- How can simplicity become a spiritual practice in your life?

- What might creation be trying to teach you today?

Porchlight Parable

Sometimes the loudest sermon is preached by a flower opening in silence.

In the quiet corners of our lives, where the hustle and bustle of the world fades to a gentle hum, nature unfolds its stories in the most profound ways. A single bloom, unfurling its petals with grace, speaks volumes about resilience and beauty. It reminds us that growth often occurs in the stillness, away from the spotlight, yet its impact is undeniably powerful.

Each petal reaches out to the light, embracing its essence, just as we too strive to grow towards our own sources of inspiration and hope.

The porchlight flickered gently, casting a warm glow over the garden, where the evening air was filled with the soft rustle of leaves and the distant song of crickets. It was a sanctuary, a place where time seemed to pause, allowing moments of reflection and gratitude to take root. Here, under the starlit sky, one could find solace in the simplicity of nature's wisdom—a reminder that every day holds the potential for quiet miracles and the beauty of beginnings anew.

11

Augustine's Porchlight
Rest for the Restless Soul

"My soul shall wait only upon God: for my expectation is from him." — Psalm 62:5 (KJV)

St. Augustine once wrote, *"Our hearts are restless until they rest in You."* That line has echoed through centuries, lighting the way for weary souls searching for peace. It's not just poetic—it's prophetic.

We chase answers. We chase approval. We chase purpose. But the porchlight of grace doesn't ask us to chase—it invites us to come home.

Rest isn't found in resolution. It's found in relationships.

The Ache of the Soul

There's a kind of tired that sleep can't fix. A kind of ache that success can't soothe. Augustine understood that. He knew that the soul was made for communion, not consumption.

I've felt that ache. In seasons of busyness. In moments of doubt. In the quiet after disappointment. And I've learned that the only cure is presence—not mine, but His.

The porch becomes a place of soul-rest. A place where striving stops and surrender begins.

Porchlight Wisdom

Augustine didn't offer easy answers. He offered honest questions. He wrestled with God, with self, with sin—and found grace not in perfection, but in pursuit.

The porchlight doesn't blind—it beckons. It's not a spotlight—it's a lamp. It says, *You're welcome here. You're safe here. You're seen here.*

And in that light, the restless heart begins to breathe again.

Timely Quotes

"You have made us for Yourself, O Lord, and our heart is restless until it rests in You." — St. Augustine

"Peace is not the absence of trouble, but the presence of Christ." — Inspired by Augustine's writings

"Rest is not escape—it's return." — Paraphrased truth

The Light That Waits

Charles E. Cravey

He searched through books and wandered far from
grace,
A scholar lost in questions of the soul.
Yet even in the darkest, deepest place,
He found a light that made the broken whole.

So too the porch, where restless hearts may land,
Where silence speaks and mercy takes its seat.
No need for answers written out by hand—
Just presence where the sacred and soul meet.

The light does not demand we come prepared,
It only asks we come with open heart.

And in that glow, the burdens we have shared
Begin to lift, and healing makes its start.

Augustine's lamp still shines through time and
space—
Inviting every soul to rest in grace.

Prayer Bench Moment

Lord, I've searched in many places,
But only You bring peace.
Let me rest not in answers,
but in Your presence.
Turn on the porchlight of grace,
and let my soul come home. Amen.

Reader Reflection

- What restlessness have you been carrying lately?

- Where have you looked for peace that didn't satisfy?

- What would it mean to rest in God—not just physically, but spiritually?

Porchlight Parable

The porchlight doesn't chase you down.
It waits—until you're ready to come home.

It stands as a silent sentinel, casting its warm glow into the night, signaling safety and comfort to those who wander. Its gentle light is a beacon of welcome, whispering promises of warmth, familiarity, and rest to the weary traveler.

The porchlight doesn't ask questions or hurry the steps; it merely offers its unwavering presence, a reminder that no matter how far we stray, there's always a place that holds our history, our stories, and our heart. This humble glow becomes a symbol of patience and understanding, ever ready to illuminate the path back to where we belong.

12

The Rhythm of
My Heart
Living in Step with Grace

"Keep thy heart with all diligence; for out of it are the issues of life." — Proverbs 4:23 (KJV)

Life has a rhythm. Not always predictable. Not always smooth. But always sacred.

There are seasons when the heart beats fast—when joy overflows and purpose pulses strong. And there are seasons when the rhythm slows—when grief settles in, when silence stretches long, when the next step feels uncertain.

But through it all, grace keeps time. The Spirit moves not in chaos, but in cadence. And the porch becomes a place where we learn to listen again.

The Pulse of Presence

I've lived through hurried seasons—where the calendar ruled and the soul was quiet. I've also lived through hollow seasons—where the silence was loud and the Spirit felt distant.

But in both, I've learned to lean into the rhythm of grace. To trust that God doesn't rush. He doesn't stall. He moves in time with love.

The porch is where I hear that rhythm best. In the creak of the rocker. In the hush of the morning. In the steady beat of a heart learning to trust again.

A Life in Step

We often try to lead the dance. But faith is about following. About letting the Spirit set the tempo. About learning to move not with fear, but with freedom.

The rhythm of my heart is not perfect. But it is present. And when it aligns with heaven's melody, even the broken beats become beautiful.

Timely Quotes

"God walks slowly because He is love." — Inspired by Japanese theologian Kosuke Koyama

"Grace has a rhythm—and it always waits for you." — Paraphrased truth

"Let your heart beat in time with eternity." — Inspired by Thomas Merton

The Beat of Grace

Charles E. Cravey

It doesn't rush, this rhythm of the soul,
Nor does it stall when sorrow dims the light.
It moves in time with mercy's quiet goal.
And dances through the day and into night.

The porch becomes a metronome of peace,
Where rocking chairs keep time with heaven's song.
And every breath becomes a sweet release,
A sacred beat that carries us along.

So let me live in step with holy sound,
Not chasing noise but listening for grace.
Let every heartbeat be where love is found.
And every pause becomes a resting place.

The rhythm of my heart is not my own—
It pulses with the One who calls me home.

Prayer Bench Moment

Lord, teach me to live in rhythm with You.

Let my heart beat not with fear,

but with faith.

Slow me down when I rush.

Lift me up when I stall.

Let my life move in time with grace. Amen.

Reader Reflection

- What rhythm has your heart been following lately?

- Where do you need to slow down and listen?

- How can you align your life with the cadence of grace?

Porchlight Parable

The heart doesn't need to race to be holy.
It just needs to beat in time with love.

Illuminated by the soft glow of the porchlight, the
evening air felt almost sacred, as if the world was
holding its breath in quiet reverence. This was a time
for gentle reflections and whispered dreams, a space
where ordinary moments became imbued with extraordinary meaning. The porch, with its creaking
wooden boards and weathered rocking chair, served
as a threshold between the mundane and the magi-
cal.

In this serene setting, hearts found solace and stories found their voice. Each heartbeat resonated with the rhythm of love, echoing tales of kindness, courage, and compassion.

The porchlight, a silent sentinel, watched over these musings, casting warm shadows that danced playfully across the walls. It was here, under its steady gaze, that the essence of holiness was felt—not in grand gestures, but in the simplicity of being present, in the quiet strength of a heart aligned with love's gentle beat.

13

Closing
Benediction
The Porch Light Still Shines

My Benediction for You, My Friend

May your porch always be a place of peace.

Where Grace rocks gently in the chair beside you.

Where welcome is wide, and judgment is absent.

Where the Spirit whispers in the breeze,

and the Gospel is served warm and sweet.

May your heart find rest—not in answers,

but in presence.

Not in perfection,

but in the One who calls you beloved.

May your story be a song of surrender,

your table a testimony of kindness,

and your life a rhythm of holy love.

And when the night grows long

and the road feels weary,

May you remember this:

The porch light still shines.

The chair still waits.

And Grace is always home.

Amen.

Other Books by Dr. Cravey may be found at:

https://drcharlescravey.com

Amazon.com/Charles Cravey Books

www.ingramcontent.com/pod-product-compliance
Lightning Source LLC
La Vergne TN
LVHW011209080426
835508LV00007B/697